More praise for *Banana Bread*

Among the important ingredients for studying Mandarin, there is the practice of play, as language study across as many chasms as exist between English and Mandarin requires many leaps of faith. What better theme than baking banana bread. The poems here are as much a display of the process of language acquisition as the generous sharing of what helped bring one poet through the havoc wreaked by COVID-19. The world survives, and so does the propensity of Scrimgeour to not only play, but to give.

— **Afaa Michael Weaver**, Author of *The Government of Nature*

香蕉面包
流行病时期中文日记

Banana Bread
Mandarin Pandemic Diary

J.D. SCRIMGEOUR

Nixes Mate Books
Allston, Massachusetts

Book design by d'Entremont
Cover photograph by karandaev, used with permission.

ISBN 978-1-949279-38-2

Nixes Mate Books
POBox 1179
Allston, MA 02134
nixesmate.pub

"A poem is my easiest homework assignment."

--Mingyue Tao

最简单的作业是一首诗

--(trans. J.D. Scrimgeour)

Contents

香蕉面包

流行病时期中文日记

Banana Bread

Mandarin Pandemic Diary

三月十三号

今天，每个人看起来很紧张。
每个人都很紧张。
没有人笑，没有人接吻。
我和我太太接吻，可是‘接’的不是‘吻。’
一些学生发短信给我：
小心，戴口罩，多睡觉。
他们的话，我看了想哭。

用中文很难。我只有一点儿话。
我有很多感情。
今天早上，我会骑车去学校。
我跟学生会聊天。我们会说英文。
然后，我跟别的学生会聊天。
我们会说中文。
我会高兴吗？不知道。
可是我会学，会感受。
今天下午我会向着太阳骑回家。

March 13

Today, everyone looks nervous.
Everyone is nervous.
No one laughed, no one kissed.
My wife and I kissed, but didn't kiss.
Some of my students texted me:
Be careful. Wear a mask. Get sleep.
I read their words and I think I may cry.

It is difficult to use Chinese.
I only have a few words. I have many feelings.
This morning, I will bike to school.
I'll talk to students. We'll speak English.
Then, I'll talk to other students.
We'll speak Chinese.
Will I be happy? I don't know.
But I can learn and think.
I will ride home to the sun this afternoon.

三月十四号

昨天我练习写中文了
我写诗了。
今天我会写另一首诗
我不知道为什么。

昨天Ming说我的诗是费纸
它让Molly悲伤。
Yicheng给我看了一部关于台湾诗人的电影。
我不应该写诗。

我应该做饭。
可是什么饭?
面包吗? 面包!
可是什么面包?

不是美国面包
不是中国面包
啊!
香蕉面包。

March 14

I practiced writing Chinese yesterday.
I wrote a poem.
Today I will write another poem.
I don't know why.

Yesterday Ming said that my poem was toilet paper.
It made Molly sad.
Yicheng showed me a movie about Taiwanese poets.
I should not write poetry.

I should bake.
But what should I bake?
Bread? Bread!
But what kind of bread?

Not American bread.
Not Chinese bread.
Ah!
Banana bread.

可是……
我不知道怎么
做香蕉面包。
我还需要老香蕉。

市场有绿色的香蕉
市场有黄色的香蕉
可是没有老香蕉。我会买
然后我和每个人会等。

But. . .
I don't know how
to bake banana bread.
Also, I need old bananas.

There are green bananas in the market.
There are yellow bananas in the market.
But there are no old bananas. I will buy bananas.
Then everyone and I will wait.

三月十五号

昨天我没有做香蕉面包
你呢？
今天我不能做香蕉面包。
我不能去学校。
我可以写诗。

我想做香蕉面包
可是我的香蕉没老
我的诗很老。
我写诗已经很多年。
岁月挂在我的诗树上。它们纷纷坠落。

岁月落在大大的香蕉面包上！
我的全部岁月离开我的诗
而今，我没有岁月。
我的诗只有几个小时，
我的香蕉面包在膨胀。

March 15

I didn't bake banana bread yesterday
Did you?
I can't bake banana bread today.
I can't go to school.
I can write poetry.

I want to bake banana bread,
but my bananas are not old.
My poem is very old.
My poem has many years in it.
They hang from my poem tree. They fall.

They fall into a giant banana bread!
All my years leave my poem.
Now, I have no years.
My poem only has a few hours.
My banana bread is rising.

三月十六号

今天，因为我是美国人
我想赚很多钱。
我想卖我的诗
可是谁喜欢买诗？
我想卖香蕉面包
可是在塞勒姆只有中国人吃它
而且他们想我免费给他们。

啊！
我会做电影
音乐的电影！
中国人在中国喜欢中文音乐
他们喜欢电影。
中国有很多中国人
他们有很多钱。

这个电影会有
鲍勃·迪伦的音乐。
中国人喜欢他的音乐。
它会有很伤心的爱情故事
它会有一个美国男生金色头发

March 16

Today, because I am American,
I want to make a lot of money.
I want to sell my poems,
but who likes to buy poetry?
I want to sell banana bread,
but in Salem, only Chinese eat banana bread,
and they want me to give it to them for free.

Ah!
I can make a movie.
A music video!
Chinese people in China like music.
They like movies.
There are many Chinese in China.
They have a lot of money.

This movie will have Bob Dylan's music.
Chinese people like his music.
It will be a very sad love story.
It will have an American boy with blond hair
singing.

在唱歌。
它会有一个中国女生
他们在分手。
女生坐着，在看海
男生在走路。
而且我们听到他唱迪伦的歌：
别想两次，没关系。

中国人会爱它！
他们会买它！
我会变得有钱！
可是我需要音乐家。
我的儿子是音乐家！
一个有一点儿金色头发的人。
可是我需要一个中国女生
谁想赚钱
而且可以演很好。
谁？谁……
我不认识像这样的人。
没关系
我不会做电影
我会写诗。
像很多美国人
我 不会变得有钱。

It will have a Chinese girl.
They are breaking up.
The girl is sitting, looking at the sea.
The boy is walking down a road.
We hear him singing Dylan in Chinese:
Don't think twice, It's alright.

Chinese people will love it!
They will buy it!
I will become rich!
But I need musicians.
My sons are musicians!
One has blond hair.
But I need a Chinese girl
who wants to make money
and can act well.
Who? Who…
I don't know anyone like this.
It's alright.
I will not make movies.
I will write poetry.
Like many Americans,
I will not become rich.

三月十七号

天是灰色
我的心不是灰色
在我的心有一颗树。
树是灰色
也有绿色。
很多灰色
小小绿芽。

你看到它们了吗？
它们像小眼睛。
它们看你
它们看到对方。
它们很小
可是它们非常绿。

它们像绿雨滴
绿眼泪
绿糖果。

March 17

The sky is grey.
My heart is not grey.
There is a tree in my heart.
The tree is grey
but also green.
A lot of grey,
a few green shoots.

Do you see them?
They are like little eyes.
They look at you.
They see each other.
They are small,
but they are very green.

They are like green raindrops,
green tears,
green candy.

三月十八号

今天晚上，飞机怒吼从黑到黑。
狗看窗外，它们不怒吼，只是看。

我们走我们城市的街上，和人们说你好。
我们的朋友远离我们，我们远离他们。

我记得我很久以前写过：
我答应给你一株植物，一首歌曲，

一个在空地方跳舞的东西
在我们的晚空里。

March 18

Tonight, a plane roars from black to black.
Dogs look out windows. They don't roar, they just look.

We walk the streets of our city and say hello.
Our friends stay away from us, we stay away from them.

I remember I wrote a long time ago:
I promise to give you a plant, a song,

something to dance in the empty place
in our evening sky.

三月十九号

我会想他们
他们会想香蕉面包
他们离开前我需要做香蕉面包。

我两个春天前在南京认识他们
第一天我的儿子丢了电话
Molly找到了它。
Yicheng不喜欢Ezra Pound
他觉得Pound不懂中文。
Ming那时候还叫Tracy
她觉得Frost的诗
需要更多的爱。

我记得晚上下课在南京的地铁站走着
觉着：它有很多意思
这些学生，这个世界。

March 19

I will miss them.
They will miss banana bread.
Before they leave, I must make banana bread.

I met them in Nanjing two springs ago.
My son lost his phone on the first day.
Molly found it.
Yicheng didn't like Ezra Pound.
He thought Pound didn't understand Chinese.
Ming called herself Tracy.
She felt Frost's poems
needed more love.

I remember walking to the subway after class
in the warm Nanjing night, feeling:
it's a lot of fun, these students, this world.

三月二十号

今天我学了中文
我学习了感情
我知道生气
我知道高兴
我知道难过
我知道紧张
我知道奇怪
我已经知道这些感情。
我大概会把它们忘记
可是今天我学到了更多。
我几乎学完了感情
明天我会学习时间。

March 20

I studied Chinese today.
I learned emotions.
I know angry.
I know happy.
I know sad.
I know nervous.
I know weird.
I already knew these feelings.
I will probably forget them,
but today I learned them more.
I'm almost finished studying feelings.
Tomorrow, I will study time.

三月二十一号

今天， 明天，
我走，我会走。
我听见很多东西
我看见很少东西
我看着香蕉变得更老
我看着树变得更年轻。
天空是一样的
蓝色，白色，灰色，黑色，
还一样。
我说：天空！
你看什么？
你的脸很漂亮
也很可怕。
我走，你看。
为什么你不走？
我会跟随你。

March 21

Today, tomorrow,
I walk, I will walk.
I hear many things.
I don't see much.
I see bananas becoming older.
I see trees becoming younger.

The sky is the same.
Blue, white, gray, black,
still the same.
I say: sky!
What do you see?
Your face is beautiful
and scary.
I walk, you look.
Why don't you walk?
I will follow you.

三月二十二号

我看得清楚
外面，一座白色的房子
一座蓝色的房子
一座白色的房子

我从我黄色的房子向外看
我们这条街上的房子比树还多
可是房子说话太少
树嘛？树说话却很多。

树和鸟讲故事
故事很奇怪
房子不笑
房子不说话。

黄色的房子！
我们的家！
笑！说话！
告诉鸟和树：

March 22

I see clearly.
Outside, a white house,
a blue house,
a white house.

I look from my yellow house.
There are more houses on our street than trees,
but the houses talk too little.
Trees? They talk a lot.

They and birds tell stories.
The stories are strange.
The houses do not laugh.
The houses do not speak.

Yellow house!
Our home!
Laugh! Speak!
Tell bird and tree

你最喜欢的故事
你最喜欢的诗。
别忘记我们都
住在这条街上。

your favorite story,
your favorite poem.
Don't forget we all live
on this street.

三月二十三号

正在下雨
还是
下雪
还是
我在下雨
还是
我在下雪—
那是什么？

我们的房子在说话。
我们的房子在说话！
我已经等了又等
现在， 我的房子说话。
我不懂我的房子
可是我听见它
所以我很高兴。
明天我会懂吗？
没关系。
它说。
我听。

March 23

It's raining
or
it's snowing
or
I'm raining
or
I'm snowing –
What's that?

Our house is talking.
Our house is talking!
I have waited and waited,
now, my house speaks.
I don't understand my house,
but I hear it,
so I am happy.
Will I understand tomorrow?
It doesn't matter.
It speaks.
I listen.

三月二十四号

我想笑
我笑
我想哭
我哭
我想吃香蕉面包
我必须等待。
我喜欢等着
当我等，我思考
我思考，我写诗。
我写关于香蕉面包的诗。
香蕉面包里有巧克力
所以我把巧克力放在我的诗里
所以我的诗变得像香蕉面包：
有巧克力
有希望
有时间
今天，我把它给你。

March 24

I want to laugh,
I laugh.
I want to cry,
I cry.
I want to eat banana bread.
I have to wait.
I like to wait.
When I wait, I think.
I think, then I write.
I write a poem about banana bread.
The banana bread has chocolate,
so I put chocolate in my poem,
so my poem becomes like banana bread:
with chocolate,
with hope,
with time.
Today, I give it to you.

三月二十五号

向谁借希望？

从黑色的鸟那里？
它们在书中
还是在树上。

从我的母亲那里？
她有希望之书
可是她需要它。

从我的父亲那里？
他有希望之树
可是他爱它。

我有一个家
它很小很温暖
我有一颗心。

它很小很温暖
我有一首诗
它很小很温暖。

March 25

Who to borrow hope from?

From the black bird?
They are in books
or in trees.

From my mother?
She has a book of hope,
but she needs it.

From my father?
He has a tree of hope,
but he loves it.

I have a home.
It is small and warm.
I have a heart

It is small and warm.
I have a poem.
It is small and warm.

黑色的鸟说：
向谁？向谁？
我说：我。

The black bird says:
Who? who?
I say: me.

三月二十七号

今天我写两首诗
一首是因为昨天我没有写
一首是因为我做了一个梦。
可不可以把一首诗变两首？
一首诗可以是一个湖泊吗？
我游泳
同时在水里也在水外
同时在水里也在水外
我游泳
一首诗可以是一个湖泊吗？
可不可以把一首诗变两首？
一首是因为我做了一个梦
一首是因为我昨天我没有写
今天我写两首诗。

March 27

Today I write two poems.
One is because I didn't write one yesterday.
One is because I had a dream.
Can one poem be two poems?
Can a poem be a lake?
I swim
Both in and out of the water
Both in and out of the water
I swim
Can a poem be a lake?
Can one poem be two poems?
One is because I had a dream.
One is because I did not write one yesterday.
Today I write two poems.

三月二十八号

晚上，我很累，
今天，我走了很远。
狗看了我
猫没看我
它们看了鸟
鸟看了地面
它们找食物
猫找食物
狗找……我不知道。
我呢？
每只狗都找我吗？
为什么？
我没有狗粮
我只是鸟
一只很累的鸟。

March 28

Night. I am very tired.
Today, I walked far.
Dogs looked at me.
Cats didn't look at me.
They looked at the birds.
The birds looked at the ground.
They look for food.
The cat looks for food.
Dogs look for. . . I don't know.
Me?
Are all dogs looking for me?
Why?
I don't have dog food.
I am just a bird,
a tired bird.

三月二十九号

雨喜欢我
雨喜欢太阳。

你不觉得雨喜欢太阳
但是它用太阳作画。

雨和太阳一起做出彩色
它们一起作画。

太阳说：不错。
雨说：我喜欢。

你在做什么？
你在给什么？

谁是你的朋友？
雨能有朋友吗？能。

雨能是你的朋友吗？
如果你听，如果你画

March 29

Rain likes me.
It likes the sun.

You don't think rain likes the sun,
but it uses the sun for painting.

Together, the rain and sun make all colors.
They paint together.

The sun says: Not bad.
The rain says: I like.

What are you doing?
What are you giving?

Who is your friend?
Can rain have friends? It can.

Can rain be your friend?
If you listen, if you paint,

如果每天你说
不错，我喜欢。.

if every day you say,
Not bad, I like.

三月三十号

太多雨了
阳光不多。
太多水了
阳光不多。
太多报纸
不多香蕉面包。

我没有香蕉面包
我喝雨。
我没有香蕉面包
我吃太阳。
我没有香蕉面包
我同风唱歌。

March 30

Too much rain,
not enough sun.
Too much water,
not enough sun.
Too many newspapers,
not enough banana bread.

I don't have banana bread.
I drink rain.
I don't have banana bread.
I eat the sun.
I don't have banana bread.
I sing with the wind.

三月三十一号

再见三月
这一年，你不好。
你不让我跟朋友见面
我只能跟我的房子说话。

我吃了很多饭
可是我没吃香蕉面包。
香蕉面包在三月没有来
它和三月不是朋友。

四月！快来！来快乐！
一个诗人说四月是最残酷的月。
它会很残酷，可是
它有太阳，有雨，它们一起作画。

我们看看, 看了又看
我们进入这个画
这个画进入我们
是香蕉面包的画。

March 31

Goodbye, March.
This year, you were not good.
You didn't let me see my friends.
I only spoke to my house.

I have eaten a lot,
but I didn't eat banana bread.
Banana bread did not come in March.
It and March are not friends.

April! Come fast! Come happy!
A poet said that April is the cruelest month.
It will be cruel, but
it has sun and rain, they paint together.

We look and look and look and look.
We enter this painting.
This painting enters us.
It is a picture of banana bread.

四月一号

每年，这天我们说谎
然后我们笑
哈哈哈。

今天我笑了
因为风笑了
风笑了
因为它能自由移动
而且因为树都笑了
它们笑了
因为风说谎。

这是今天的歌
哈哈哈。
我们一起唱歌吧
你，我，风，树
哈哈哈
哈哈哈。

April 1

Every year on this day we lie
then we laugh.
Hahaha.

I laughed today
because the wind laughed.
The wind laughed
because it can move freely
and because the trees laughed.
They laughed
because the wind lies.

This is today's song,
Hahaha.
Let's sing together
you, me, wind, tree,
Hahaha
Hahaha.

四月二号

当我们结婚时
我们很新。
我们的眼睛很新
我们的脸很新
我们觉得：世界非常老
可是我们将永远很新。
我们当时不知道。

我们觉得：世界爱我们
因为我们爱世界
可是世界不认识我们。
以前我们问：为什么世界
背负这么多悲伤？
现在我们问：为何换我们背负？

April 2

When we got married
we were very new.
Our eyes were new.
Our faces were new.
We felt: the world is very old,
but we will always be new.
We didn't know.

We felt: the world loved us
because we loved the world.
But the world didn't know us.
We asked: why did the world
carry so much sorrow?
Now we ask: why do we?

四月三号

我看春天
我看你
你看不看我？
我穿着雨
我穿着你的希望
它在我身上很好看
它闪耀。

我需要穿别人的希望。
有的时候我不想
穿别人的东西
可是春天里
总是有别人
而我总是
想穿春天。

April 3

I see spring.
I see you.
Do you see me?
I am wearing rain.
I am wearing your hope.
It looks good on me.
It shines.

I need to wear others' hope.
Sometimes I don't want
to wear other people's things,
but in spring,
there are always other people,
and I always want
to wear spring.

四月十六号

美国人说：我们喜欢变化
我们不喜欢历史，不学它
艺术？我们不在乎
诗歌？哈哈哈

我们找新门
我们开新门
我们开新车
我们吃新饭。

我们住在新里
新新新
新住在心里
等等，别人说，你们有心吗？

April 16

Americans say: We like change.
We don't like history and don't learn it.
Art? We don't care.
Poetry? Hahaha.

We look for new doors.
We open them.
We drive new cars.
We eat new food.

We live new.
New new new.
New is in our hearts.
Wait, others say, you have a heart?

四月十八号

今天没有变化，
我走了路，我看了电脑
我吃了饭，没有变化，没有新事物。
我想……离家吗？
不想。
我想睡觉吗？
我想，可是我老是睡觉。

我的朋友喜欢香蕉面包
他们对我说：请做香蕉面包
我们必须有它。你做面包，就现在！
我喜欢我的朋友，我喜欢香蕉面包。
我会做的！变化会来！
我们都会吃香蕉面包
而且我们会很高兴。

April 18

Today, nothing changed.
I walked, I looked at the computer,
I ate. No change, nothing new.
Do I want to. . . leave the house?
I don't.
Do I want to sleep?
I do, but I always sleep.

My friends like banana bread.
They asked me: Please bake banana bread.
We must have it. You bake it. Now!
I like my friends. I like banana bread.
I will do it! Change will come!
We will all eat banana bread,
and we will be happy.

四月十九号

今天很漂亮
可是今天是四月十九号。
四月十九号在美国
发生了很多坏事。
每个四月十九号我都害怕
可是今天很漂亮。
我见了我的中国朋友
我们看了大海
我们做了小电影
我给了他们香蕉面包
他们给我奶黄包。

看大海很好
给予，吃，创造
我更懂了这个日子
我更懂了时间。

April 19

Today is beautiful,
but today is April 19th.
A lot of bad things have happened
in the United States on April 19th.
Every April 19th I am afraid,
but today is beautiful.
I saw my Chinese friends.
We looked at the sea.
We made a small movie.
I gave them banana bread.
They gave me steamed custard buns.

It's good to see the sea,
to give, to eat, to create.
I understand this day more.
I understand time more.

四月二十五号

太阳甩了我们。
我们说：太阳！
为什么您不回来？
您找一个新世界吗？
在哪儿？我每天寻找它。
我只找到这个旧世界
它很湿，它很冷
这里每个人都很累。
太阳！带我进入新世界！
我不会告诉任何人。

我想知道它在哪儿
我想知道它是真的
我想知道您
请让我。
我会给您这世界
最后一朵花
它是灰色的
可是最漂亮。

April 25

The sun broke up with us.
We say: Sun!
Why don't you return?
Are you looking for a new world?
Where? I look for it every day.
I only find this old world.
It's very wet, it's very cold.
Everyone here is tired.
Sun! Take me into the new world!
I will not tell anyone.

I want to know where it is.
I want to know it is.
I also want to know you.
Please let me.
I will give you from this world
the last flower.
It is gray,
but it is the most beautiful.

五月三号

今天，我的生日。
早上，我的太太在睡觉
我的儿子在睡觉。
我吃了一个甜甜圈
我喝了我的咖啡
现在我写一点儿汉字。
太阳说：你好，小男人
你过得好吗？

太阳，我说，每年都好
每年都不好。我多知道一点儿
我多忘掉一点儿。
每年你说：你好，小男人
当我听到您的声音
我觉得不小。

May 3

Today. My birthday.
Morning. My wife is sleeping.
My son is sleeping.
I ate a donut.
I had my coffee.
Now I write a few Chinese characters.
The sun says: Hello, little man,
how have you been?

Sun, I say, every year is good,
every year is not so good. I know a little more,
I forget a little more.
Every year you say: Hello, little man,
and when I hear you,
I feel big.

五月十五号

昨天晚上，大风暴
今天早上，太阳
新太阳，许多鸟。

我知道很多树都受伤了
它们躺在街上，它们像老人。

昨晚我只睡了一点儿觉
我看了我的日记
我记得了我忘掉的中国字。
我记得了三月
我记得了四月。

现在邻居的黑猫已经在狩猎
鸟小心吧，我小心吧。
我记得。我忘掉。
黑猫像雨水一样消失。

May 15

Last night, there was a huge storm.
This morning, sun.
New sun. Many birds.

I know many trees are injured.
They lie on the street. They are like old people.

I slept a little last night.
I read my diary.
I remembered the Chinese characters I'd forgotten.
I remembered March,
I remembered April.

Now the neighbor's black cat is already hunting.
Birds, be careful. J.D., be careful.
I remember. I forget.
The black cat, like rain, disappears.

Acknowledgments

My month in China in Spring 2018 changed my life. I taught poetry to a group of students at Nanjing Normal University who would come to Salem State that fall for two years of study, and I met the Chair of their English Department, Emma Zhu. How big the world became; how small was I.

Back in the United States, I began translating contemporary Chinese poetry with some of those students. Early in the pandemic, when we suddenly could no longer meet in person, I started writing diary entries in Mandarin to practice my fledgling skills in the language. The entries turned into poems, which I translated into English. Then, with my students' help, I fine-tuned both the Mandarin and the English within the constraints of limited vocabulary and syntax. The results are as much acts of language acquisition as poems, but maybe that's what all poems are.

Thanks to my first Mandarin teacher, Ti-cheng Balbo.
Thanks to Eileen FitzGerald, James and Christine Scrimgeour, Afaa Michael Weaver, and Emma Zhu for reading the manuscript and offering encouragement.

Thanks to Michael McInnis and Nixes Mate for believing in the work and making it shine.

Thanks to Zhang Ziqing for his generous reading and editing of the Mandarin.

Thanks to the Chinese poetry translation group: MP Carver, Greg Glenn, Xinrui Jiang, Yezhen Ma, Yangxu Shen, Yicheng Tao, and Zhen Xu.

And special thanks to a member of that group and my Chinese tutor, Mingyue Tao, who spent many hours on Zoom revising the Mandarin with me, making sure it kept all the awkward locutions of a beginner while also being comprehensible. In many ways, she's a co-author of this work.

Poems from this collection originally appeared in the following magazines:
Poetry Sky: March 13, March 18, April 3, May 15
On the Seawall: March 13, March 19, March 20, April 2, May 3, May 15
New World Poetry (Chinese versions only): "三月十三号," "三月十八号," "四月三号," "五月十五号."

About the Author

J.D. Scrimgeour is the author of four poetry collections *The Last Miles*, *Territories*, *Lifting the Turtle*, and *Festival*. He won the AWP Award for Nonfiction for his second book of nonfiction, *Themes for English B: A Professor's Education In & Out of Class*. With musician Philip Swanson he released *Ogunquit & Other Works*, a CD blending music and poetry. The musical, *Only Human*, which he composed with his sons Aidan and Guthrie, premiered at Ames Hall Theatre in Salem in 2014. He is Chair of Salem State University's English Department.

A longtime resident of Salem, he's written in many genres about the city. Mary Towne Eastey, an ancestor in his direct line, was put to death during the Salem Witch Trials. Another ancestor, Thomas Perkins, sat on the jury that found her guilty.

http://jdscrimgeour.com

Recent Titles from Nixes Mate

Dog-Walking In The Shadow Of Pyongyang · Devon Balwit

2 a.m. With Keats · Eileen Cleary

Nike Adjusting Her Sandal · Anastasia Vassos

FLY COTTON CHAPBOOK SERIES

The Passion of John Eliot · Michael McInnis

Chernobyl · Anne Pluto

Torero · Gloria Monaghan

Dear Teilhard, · Hannah Larrabee

Lose Sight of Heaven · Zofia Provizor

Innocents · Cindy Veech

In the Year of Ferraro · Jennifer Martelli

42° 19' 47.9" N 70° 56' 43.9" W

Nixes Mate is a navigational hazard in Boston Harbor used during the colonial period to gibbet and hang pirates and mutineers.

Nixes Mate Books features small-batch artisanal literature, created by writers who use all 26 letters of the alphabet and then some, honing their craft the time-honored way: one line at a time.

nixesmate.pub

www.ingramcontent.com/pod-product-compliance
Ingram Content Group UK Ltd.
Pitfield, Milton Keynes, MK11 3LW, UK
UKRC032233290726
14090UKWH00009B/494